Praise for the Dating Goddess

The *Adventures in Delicious Dating After 40* series of books is based on the blog Adventures in Delicious Dating After 40 at www.DatingGoddess.com. Here are comments from readers.

💜 "Adventures in Delicious Dating After 40 is a wonderful composite of both the mechanics of post-40 online dating and what the practice of honoring one's self actually looks like. How marvelous your writing is to read. I spent about 2 hours reading and was riveted the whole time." —Maggie Hanna

💜 "At last, a dating writer who addresses requirements. You are SO right on! I'm thrilled to have found you!" —Rachel Sarah, author, *Single Mom Seeking*

💜 "Powerfully heartfelt and honest writing. You are inspiring." —Kare Anderson, Emmy Award winning writer

i

💟 "I just love your writing. It is very fresh and gives the reader something to think about." —Kelly Lantz, President & Manager, 55-Alive.com

💟 "Dating Goddess, you are like a, a, a, well, a goddess to me. You've helped guide me successfully through my re-entry into the dating world after 14 years. I'm an eager student and fast study, and do get myself into situations that others don't know how to deal with — such as 3 dates in one day -— so thankfully you are there! You're the greatest, thanks for all you do for us!" —Jae G.

💟 "I find your point of view much more interesting than other dating writers. Thanks for always reminding me to enjoy dating life no matter what it throws at you." —Sandy

💟 "I love Adventures in Delicious Dating After 40. I really do like your honest and authentic voice — it's refreshing." —Wendy S.

💟 "Adventures in Delicious Dating After 40 is really fun to read. Thanks for sharing your thoughts and letting us divorced single women know that we are not alone. There's a lot here that I identify with, although I'm not as brave as you are about dating lots of guys. So far. Love your blog — the first blog I've ever read consistently." —Elizabeth

💟 "Thanks for a wonderful blog. You're doing a great job of saying what's in my mind. There's rarely a day I miss when it comes to checking in on your wisdom." —Paulette Ensign

Multidating Responsibly

*Play the Field
Without Being A Player*

by **Dating Goddess**

Multidating Responsibly: Play the Field Without Being A Player

Second Edition

Cover design by Dave Innis, www.innisanimation.com

Book design by JustYourType.biz

Printed in the United States of America.

ISBN   Print: 978-1-930039-93-3

eBook: 978-1-930039-20-9

How to order:

The *Adventures in Delicious Daing After 40* books may be ordered directly from www.DatingGoddess.com.

Quantity discounts are also available. Visit us online for updates and additional articles.

The Adventures in Delicious Dating After 40 books are dedicated to my ex-husband since he unexpectedly released me to explore the untethered life of a single woman. I then had the freedom for the experiences, lessons and insights shared in these pages.

Books by Dating Goddess

💜 *Date or Wait: Are You Ready for Mr. Great?*

💜 *Assessing Your Assets: Why You're A Great Catch*

💜 *In Search of King Charming: Who Do I Want to Share My Throne?*

💜 *Embracing Midlife Men: Insights Into Curious Behaviors*

💜 *Dipping Your Toe in the Dating Pool: Dive In Without Belly Flopping*

💜 *Winning at the Online Dating Game: Stack the Deck in Your Favor*

💜 *Check Him Out Before Going Out: Avoiding Dud Dates*

💜 *First-Rate First Dates: Increasing the Chances of a Second Date*

💜 *Real Deal or Faux Beau: Should You Keep Seeing Him?*

💜 *Multidating Responsibly: Play the Field Without Being A Player*

💜 *Moving On Gracefully: Break Up Without Heartache*

💜 *From Fear to Frolic: Get Naked Without Getting Embarrassed*

💜 *Ironing Out Dating Wrinkles: Work Through Challenges Without Getting Steamed*

Contents

Introduction

This book is designed for anyone who is interested in stories, advice, and lessons from the midlife dating front. If you are over 40 and haven't dated in a while — or even if you have — you'll learn ways to approach dating with zeal, optimism, and hope. Even if you've had more than your share of negative experiences, I'll share how to glean lessons from those adventures, rather than just declaring that "all men are jerks" or "men are just looking for sex."

While most of the perspective is from a woman to women, men's comments, experiences, and lessons have been integrated as appropriate.

This book began as daily entries into my blog, Adventures in Delicious Dating After 40, which has been featured in the *Wall Street Journal* as well as on radio and TV. I wrote about my epiphanies from my and my friends' dating life. The best postings were culled to make this and subsequent books.

This book focuses on how to date around responsibly and with integrity without leading men on. If you do it with honesty, you can date several people at once until you're both ready to focus only on each other.

This book consists of three types of perspectives:

💜 ***Lessons:*** These are specific experiences I thought would be useful to you. A few lines from my experience illustrate the points.

💜 ***Insights:*** These usually start with an experience I've encountered, then the insights that experience spawned. It is usually comprised of around half story and half insight.

💜 ***Stories:*** These are examples of situations I've experienced — or was currently experiencing when I wrote that piece — that I thought would be entertaining. Or I thought the story would help you see what kind of things happen in the midlife dating world so you'd know what has happened to others.

Because these writings were real time, as they occured, they are often set in the present tense. But they are not chronological. So a reference to "my current beau" may now be many sweethearts ago. I hope this isn't confusing.

I'd love ot hear your stories and questions. Please email them to me at Goddess@DatingGoddess.com. They may make it into the blog or my next book!

Who is the Dating Goddess?

am a middle-aged, white, professional woman. My husband of nearly 20 years left me in April 2003 when I was 47, 11 days shy of 48. After giving my heart time to heal from the surprise divorce sprung by the man I thought was my soulmate, I started dating 18 months later. Generally, I have had a great time meeting interesting men, some of whom became romantic beaus, some became treasured friends, and some I never heard from again.

> *I am not a well-preserved, gorgeous, marathon-running middle-aged women*

In the beginning, I had dates with single male colleagues, but I quickly found Internet dating was the way to explore the most "inventory" and qualify men who I thought might be a good match.

I am not one of those well-preserved, gorgeous,

marathon-running middle-aged women. I have been told I am attractive, but I am overweight and not a gym rat. So while I am active, I do not match the description 90% of men's profiles say they want: slender, athletic, toned, fit. I have some wrinkles — what one sweet suitor mistakenly called dimples. I have what Bridget Jones called "wobbly bits," as most non-surgically enhanced middle-aged women do. My genes — and a lifetime addiction to chocolate — have made their mark. Yet I've met and dated some wonderful men, so even if you're not a lingerie model, you can find guys who will think you're attractive, perhaps even hot!

In my professional life, I am a bestselling author of workplace effectiveness books, professional speaker and management consultant. I've appeared on Oprah, 60 Minutes, and National Public Radio and in the *Wall Street Journal* and *USA Today.*

This book is intended to not only be useful to others and cathartic for me, but is also the genesis of a new topic for fun, thought-provoking speeches. I'm calling myself a dating philosopher and giving date-a-vational speeches! Let me know if you know a group who would like an entertaining after-lunch speech on how lessons learned from dating have implications in business and personal relationships and well as life philosophies.

How did I come by the Dating Goddess moniker? After a few months of dating dozens of men — one week yielded 7 dates with 6 guys in 5 days — my friends dubbed me this name. I liked it, so it stuck.

I'm purposefully not sharing my picture as I don't want you to think either, "How did she get any dates at all?" or the opposite, "Of course she found it easy to get 112 men to ask her out." I am not hideous (usually) nor am I stunning (without professional hair, makeup and Photoshop!). Some men find me attractive, some don't.

I continue to search for my "one," but I have learned a lot along the way, and my single and not-single friends have loudly encouraged me to share my experiences and lessons in the hopes of helping others navigate the adventure of dating with more success. And to have a delicious time doing it!

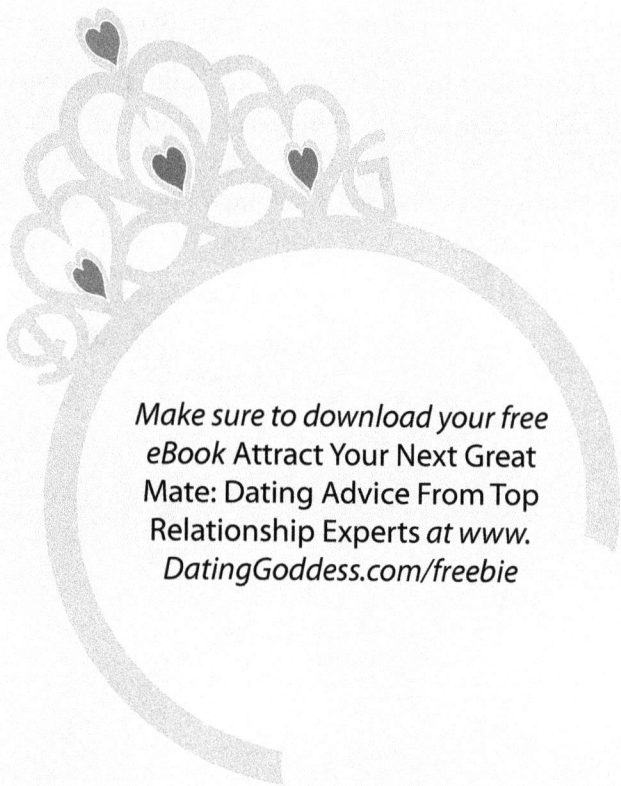

Make sure to download your free eBook Attract Your Next Great Mate: Dating Advice From Top Relationship Experts *at www. DatingGoddess.com/freebie*

"Pimpin'" — Dating multiple guys

"Save a boyfriend for a rainy day — and another, in case it doesn't rain." —Mae West

I've found that successful dating requires juggling several men at once. It is like sales — you have to have a number of prospects in the pipeline. I frequently date several men in the same time period until two of us decide to be exclusive or one of us decides to move on. If you only date one at a time, it takes too long to get the next one in the pipeline.

When I was explaining this to my teenaged nieces, they said I was "pimpin'." Now hold your hat — their definition of a pimp is not the same as mine. It merely means dating around. Let's be clear here that *dating* around does not mean *sleeping* around. You can date multiple people and not sleep with any of them. In fact, I'd recommend you not sleep with any of them until you decide to be exclusive and you both agree that means letting go of all the others you've been seeing. It is not wise or safe to be a "player."

You have to remember other details that each one

has shared, otherwise you'll ask the same things over again and he'll think you didn't pay any attention at all. Track this in your Date-A-Base (see page 7).

You need to have the discipline to not talk about your other guys while on a date. This is déclassé. While you can imply that you are seeing others, don't throw it in his face. He may think you are slutty.

But dating around gives you an opportunity to have multiple activity needs met. One likes foreign films, another opera. One likes to hike, another is a tennis buff.

You can imply that you are seeing others

He may be dating around, too. (See "Assume there are other women," page 17.) Clarify this on the first few dates just to be sure you're on the same page. When I do this, I always ask if he's sleeping with anyone. Multiple sex partners increase the risk of STDs. I recommend not sleeping with anyone until you've decided to be exclusive. Then you both get tested for STDs before going further.

Dating around has its pros and cons. I find the pros outweigh the cons. It takes special skills. You have to remember the guy's name when you're with him, unlike the time halfway through dinner that I couldn't think of my date's name (it was a first date).

Multi-dating pros
and cons

W hen I've shared with single, dating guy pals that I'm multi-dating they say that there is a double standard. If a guy talked about having dates with multiple women, he'd be chastised and accused of being a player. Women know there are unflattering terms for them as well.

Isn't the reason for dating to find out who you click with and who you don't? Sometimes you have to go through a stream of single coffee dates to find someone with whom you want to have a second date — and who wants to see you again. Is it wrong to have a second date the same week you are having a first date with someone else?

In *Date like a Man: What Men Know about Dating and Are Afraid You'll Find Out*, authors Myreah Moore and Jodie Gould share that there is nothing wrong with seeing several people at once — as long as you don't lead them to think they are the only one. Men have been doing this for centuries and have earned titles like "ladies' man," "Casanova," "playboy," "Don Juan," "lover boy," and "lady killer." Most of these terms are said with a smile and twinkle, even though some may get some negative feedback, like my male pals mentioned earlier.

A woman who multi-dates — let alone hot bunks (see page 11) — is called by different terms: "hussy," "tart," "trollop," "hoochie mama," "easy," "floozy," "tramp," "tease," "femme fatale," "seductress," "temptress," "siren," "enchantress," "vamp," "man-eater," "home wrecker" and the now popular, "ho." I couldn't come up with a positive term for a woman who dates around. Perhaps

We'll just call her smart!

we are ahead of society, so no term has been developed! I think we'll just call her smart!

One of the issues with dating multiple men is when to let them know. While it would seem best to tell him even before a face-to-face, it seems awkward.

Recently, a guy handled this well. In his first email to me he said, "It is only fair for you to know that I am actively dating others. This however does not alter my interest in finding closeness with you, but don't get mad at me if I don't propose to you over our first coffee."

Since I, too, am dating others, I appreciated his candor. I found it refreshing he was so upfront.

Another man told me on the first date he was seeing others. Again, I thought he handled it well. He told me he was attracted to me and needed to let me know he was just starting to date after his divorce, so was seeing a few other woman.

I never lie to a man, but I also don't like to rub it in his face if I'm seeing others. I drop hints that I am seeing others, and if things heat up, I will be explicit then.

Players date others but do not let you know. They would try to hide their involvement, lying and covering up. So you can see others with impunity as long as you are open about it and it is okay with the guys.

Your Date-A-Base — tracking multiple suitors

When people hear that I've dated 112 men in 3.5 years and that I often date several guys at a time, they commonly ask, "How do you keep them straight?"

I respond, "With a Date-A-Base."

Since I'm a business woman, I've long kept a database to track my customers. In business it is also known as a Customer Relationship Manager (CRM). I've adapted my business CRM to my dating life.

In my Date-A-Base, I keep track of the man's name, email, phone numbers, address, and picture. I copy his online profile into the electronic file. And I update it after we talk and I learn important things. This prevents me from asking again where he grew up, his family details, kids' names and ages, alma mater, favorite hobbies, food, books, movies, etc. I review my notes before

I know we'll be talking again.

I start a database file as soon as we go from email to the phone. I enter as much info as I have at the moment and add to it.

When you have several people you're contacting, it takes some organization to keep them all straight. Some people use a spreadsheet to track their potential dates before meeting. My friend George, also a businessman/salesman, kept a pre-date spread sheet to track info on each woman with whom he was communicating. His was similar to how he'd track his prospects and customers. He'd log where she lived, if she was divorced or separated, how many kids and their ages, who initiated contact and when, and when they'd talked by phone. He'd enter her screen name, height and age, general looks (based on her picture) and "overall plus/minus" comments.

It takes organization to keep them all straight

Other people say they use index cards to keep people's details straight. Others just print out the profile and make needed notes on it. I'm a tech-savvy gal so prefer the electronic version.

Some of my dating friends have taken this tracking spreadsheet to the next level. They have a number of categories across the top (looks, energy, intelligence, humor, etc.) and their dates' names down the side. They then assign a number from 1-10 for each of the characteristics for that person. It seems cold, doesn't it? But we all do that to some degree or another, just not so methodically. Then they can analytically decide if they want to continue seeing the person. I trust my gut more than my head, so this method wouldn't work for me.

The important point is do something to keep everyone sorted out. It's embarrassing to say, "Will you be seeing your parents for the holidays?" when his parents are deceased. Or, "I hope Stanford whips CAL" when he's a Berkeley alumnus.

"Hot bunking" your beaus

The original phrase "hot bunking" relates to sleeping in shifts on a ship. There aren't enough bunks, so one sailor gets up and another, just getting off duty, lies down before the other's body heat dissipates.

I'm using the term tongue-in-cheek here, not literally! By "hot bunking" I'm referring to those days when you have a date with more than one guy. One gal pal shared she had 3 dates with 3 guys in one day! Wow! And I thought I once had a busy week going on seven dates with six guys in five days!

> *"Hot bunking" is when you have a date with more than one guy*

The secret to hot bunking is to plan the dates with enough time in between so you aren't looking worriedly at your watch if the waiter is slow. So have a lunch date and a late-afternoon coffee date, or a drink after work. Or a morning coffee date and an afternoon one. Don't try to do a coffee date right before lunch, unless you've told him you have a lunch engagement so must leave by a certain time. And don't schedule two dates in the same restaurant, as the second might be early as you're hugging the first one goodbye! In the same mall is fine, but you do run the risk of date #1 lingering to shop and running into you with date #2.

The other secret is to review the details of #2 right before you meet, so you don't get his details intertwined with #1. I bring a printout of #2s profile with me and any notes I've taken from phone conversations. I review them before I meet #2.

And if they do happen to cross over — you run into #1 in the mall while walking with #2 to Starbucks — just be cool. If you see #1 don't try to hide, although sometimes a quick duck in a store with #2 may be the best move. But if you know he saw you, make eye contact, smile, wave, and if you speak, introduce them to each other briefly, but don't linger. Hopefully, #2 won't be hanging all over you, so you don't need to explain who he is. And exit quickly, so neither one asks the other, "So how do you know this hottie?" If you handle it coolly, they might see they aren't alone pursuing you and need to act quickly to win your heart.

Are you a "Let's Make a Deal" type of dater?

o you remember the TV show, "Let's Make a Deal"? TV.com describes it as "a game of intuition, skill, luck, decision making and greed — all mixed into one." Sounds like dating, doesn't it? Maybe not the greed part, unless a gold digger is involved.

I was thinking about this show as I was comparing several men I'd met online and deciding who to release and who to keep seeing. It reminded me of host Monty Hall offering contestants the opportunity to trade their winnings for whatever was behind doors number 1, 2 or 3. Often they didn't know what their current prize was. Nor did they know what was hidden behind various doors, boxes and curtains being offered for exchange. Monty made the choice harder by sharing the big prize but not which door it was behind. Maybe it was behind the door you chose.

13

Or perhaps it would be a "zonk" — giant shoes, a goat, rusting 19th-century appliances, a washtub for each day of the week, 1 ton of watermelons, a giant rocking horse, sequin-covered garbage cans, etc.

So it is with dating. When dating someone early on, you really don't know what "prize" you have in hand as you don't yet know him very well. But the siren call of the never-ending stream of online potential suitors is alluring. Interesting men regularly appear in your in-box winking, flirting, or emailing. At some point you have to decide whether to keep the "prize" you already have or exchange him for a tempting, but unknown, "prize." Or at least he appears tempting behind the email veil. Occasionally, he's a zonk.

The siren call of the never-ending stream of online potential suitors is alluring

That is why some of us multi-date. Then we can take a peek at both (or more) prizes simultaneously. You can see which one is most valuable (most like what you want) before you let go of the lesser-desirable one.

I know, this is offensive to some people. They feel you don't really give one guy a chance if you are seeing two (or more) concurrently. Some feel you are trying to have your cake and eat it too. Some label a woman who multi-dates as slutty.

Since I do it, I don't think it's offensive or slutty. It is a form of hedging your bets. A savvy gambler always hedges her bets so she is more likely to take home some winnings rather than wager on only one option and leave empty handed. Unless she feels it is a sure bet — which is when you decide a man has the potential to be a long-term partner. Then you don't bet on others.

Are you a "Let's Make a Deal" type of dater? Do you balance two or more men to hedge your bets? If not, what is your feeling about those who do?

Assume there are other women

Most of us who employ online dating adopt a "don't ask, don't tell" philosophy about dating multiple people simultaneously, at least until we're ready to get more serious.

When I am seeing a few guys, I don't ask the date I'm with if he's seeing others because I don't want him asking me. I assume he is, and I make decisions about how close to get to him based on that assumption. If he asks me if I'm seeing others, I'll tell him the truth. I'll then ask him.

Why don't I want him asking, at least in the early few dates? Because I don't want him to say he's not dating others and he wants us to be exclusive. Although I'm honest, it's a difficult conversation to have if he is a one-woman-at-a-time guy and I'm not ready to reciprocate. Some men don't date much, and they don't have as many options as you might. You don't want to limit your activities too early, before you've decided you want to focus on him.

I don't believe many midlife men have the organizational skills or time to see more than one woman concurrently. They are busy with work, hobbies, and perhaps kids, and for many of them to squeeze in time to see one woman is difficult, let alone two or more. My friend Bruce thinks I am naive. He says most men can balance more than one woman without a lot of trouble. Women forgive them for not remembering details of their lives. So they don't put much effort into where a woman's parents live, where she grew up, her best friend's name, etc.

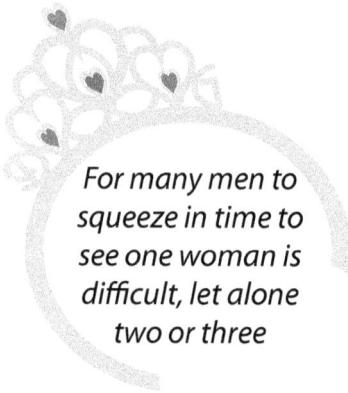

> *For many men to squeeze in time to see one woman is difficult, let alone two or three*

I discovered a guy I was dating was still seeking others by seeing that he'd logged on to the dating site within the last day or two. He could see my activity as well. Since we hadn't promised exclusivity, it wasn't a problem, but it did let me know he wasn't focused only on me. It also said he wasn't completely happy with our relationship so was hunting.

One guy was so brazen he used my laptop to log onto his Match.com account in the kitchen while I was fixing him dinner! That was tacky! It triggered an interesting discussion about where each of us was about exclusivity.

Be careful how you ask the question. If you say, "Are

you seeing anyone else?" he can honestly say "no" if he is not actually dating anyone else. However, he could be in heavy flirt mode by phone or email with one or more women, and he just hasn't had a date with them yet. So even though there's no one else at the moment you asked, that could change tomorrow after he's set up dinner with another gal. If it's important to you that he's seeing only you, in addition to the question above, ask, "Do you plan to date others while seeing me? Do you plan to contact others while we are in this exploratory stage? How are you responding to emails from others? Do you believe in dating several women simultaneously?" The challenge is to elicit the information without it seeming like an interrogation.

My philosophy is to not bring up the conversation, but to continue to meet others until he asks me about exclusivity. If you ask him, some men feel it is a noose tightening around their neck. If you want to set some parameters around physical activities until there is exclusivity, tell him so. It will have him assess how serious he is about you.

Don't ever assume you are the only one unless you've had a candid conversation with your guy.

Make sure to download your free eBook Attract Your Next Great Mate: Dating Advice From Top Relationship Experts *at www. DatingGoddess.com/freebie*

Dating's revolving door

Some of my friends tease me about the revolving door of my dating life. It is true that men come and go through my life, some rather quickly, others lingering longer. (See "They come, they go" in the *Moving On Gracefully: Break Up Without Heartache* book.)

My pals have asked "Why? Why don't more men stick around?" Good question. Some have. But I think I've become more discerning, so after a few dates I am a better judge about whether someone has stickiness or not.

Recently, after six times together, I decided that someone wasn't for me. His conversation revealed more paranoid and limited thinking than I like being around. There had been hints of that before, but in the sixth encounter it was solidified. So it was time to release him to hook up with someone more on his wavelength.

That's how it happens. One or both of us decide the other isn't right, and we let the other go, ideally with no hard feelings. Just, "We aren't a match." And hopefully, "I wish you well."

And soon another enters the turnstile.

How long do you hedge your bet?

You've been seeing someone casually, once a week for a month. You like him, and he seems to like you, as he keeps asking you to lunch and ending each encounter with a passionate kiss. He calls you a few times a week and engages in an IM chat at least once a day.

You're not smitten with him, but you like him. He's intelligent, funny, attentive, self-aware, doesn't press himself on you physically beyond the kiss, talks about waiting to get sexual until the time is right. Great, huh?

But meanwhile you continue to accept other invitations. Most are just one-time coffee meetings with nice guys but not any mutual spark.

Then — wham — a new guy comes on the scene that takes you aback. You have two dates, then due to scheduling mismatches a week passes. He calls you several times a day and tells you how much he likes you. You like him, too, in a different way than the aforementioned guy.

But you've had this happen before. Part of you feels like you should tell the first guy that you've met someone new, but you also know that New Guy could go poof any time.

How long can you have your feet in both camps? It's not like you're longing for one when you're with the other. If you were, the decision would be easy. Neither of them knows there are others, as things haven't heated up enough for that to seem relevant.

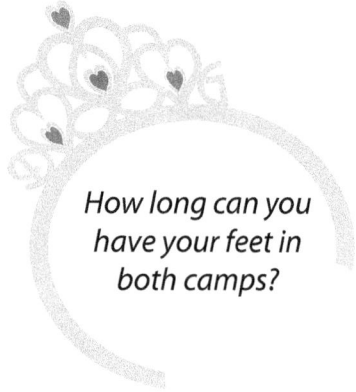

How long can you have your feet in both camps?

My rule of thumb is: when things look like they will heat up, that is the time to decide, ideally beforehand, not afterward. Then you'll be thinking with your brain, not other parts of your body. You tell one that you need to let him go, as you don't want to be intimately involved with two at once — this would not be good for anyone.

Don't hedge too long, or the second in line will feel used. You know how you'd feel if someone strung you along. As I mentioned in "Dating with integrity" (in the *Dipping Your Toe in the Dating Pool: Dive In Without Belly Flopping* book), it is sometimes hard to be 100% honest if you want to be sensitive to someone's feelings. And while most who've dated online for long understand there will be others vying for your attention during the initial stages of getting to know each other, after seeing each other a while, it's important to let someone go who you think isn't a good match. The hard part is when you are dating two people you think are both a good match. The deciding is difficult.

What are your guidelines for when to let someone go if you've been seeing two people concurrently? How long will you see both before forcing yourself to make a decision?

Beware of multi-tasking when multi-dating

When friends learn I have sometimes dated multiple men simultaneously, they ask how I am able to do so.

I can go from a conversation with one man to another pretty easily. It makes me realize how quickly we vilify those who date around, saying, "How could he take one woman out to dinner one night and another the next?" We call these people "players" even if there is no purposeful behavior to lead one to believe you are committed to them.

I now understand how men — who we stereotypically think of when we think of multidating — can go from woman to woman in a short period of time. Compartmentalizing is not that hard. I've been known to carry on two IM conversations simultaneously and not miss a beat. Or have lunch with one guy and dinner with another on the same day.

Even though I can multitask while multidating, generally, successful multidating means you have to pay attention to each man in turn. If you let your focus wane while conversing with him, he may say something that he expects you to know later. You'll have to fake it or admit you don't remember, even though it might only be hours later.

And you not only have to remember what he says — you have to be present to whom you told what. This prevents you from retelling a story to the same guy.

The difference in multidating and playing is how far one goes. The more physical or verbal affection that is expressed, the more committed the other feels you are, even if that is not explicit. And undisclosed sleeping around is generally considered not acceptable in the midlife dating world, even assuming safe sex precautions. (If only there were emotional condoms — protection to safeguard one's heart.)

If only there were emotional condoms — protection to safeguard one's heart

They key, I believe, is not to claim exclusivity or make statements that would make him believe you are seeing only him. Ideally, you state even before meeting or in the first two

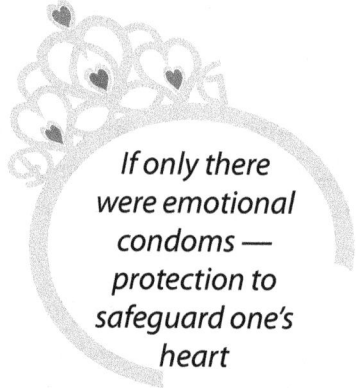

dates that you are seeing others. But if you aren't seeing others at that time, and soon someone comes along you want to get to know, it is awkward to go to the first guy and say, "By the way, I'm also getting to know another guy." Which of course, makes a mess if he assumes you are seeing only him and you're not. But the second could easily fizzle after a few phone calls or a lunch date where you clearly see you're not a good match.

I wish I could offer watertight rules for successfully multidating. Mostly, I've learned to not lead someone on with talk that makes him think you are devoted only to him, and not sleep with someone while you are seeing others or are still open to other invitations.

Back burner beaus

An Adventures in Dating After 40 reader wrote:

I recently jointly decided to be exclusive with a man I've been dating for a little while. However, I'd been multi-dating and although I've told the others I'm going to focus on one man right now, several are interested in my letting them know if it doesn't work out.

How do you deal with dangling men who are waiting in the wings? Do you still respond to their calls, emails, IMs and/or texts, even though they have dialed back their flirting and wooing? Am I cheating on my guy if I stay in touch with these guys who are now somewhere between friend and suitor? I'm not sure where the line is between appropriate pal contact and kinda dating? I'd be mortified if my guy thought I was two-timing him.

This is a very good question. I've run up against this myself, and it is hard to know what is right.

You have to ask yourself why you want to keep in touch with these guys. Are they your spares in case your #1 guy doesn't work out? Do you harbor some desire to see if they are better than the guy you've decided to focus on? Might you not give your current guy as much of a chance if you know you have fallback options waiting a phone call away?

If your decision to keep in contact is as insurance, then it's not really being fair to anyone. They keep some hope alive that you may give them a second chance to earn your attention. Your guy doesn't get your full focus, as you know you have others waiting in case he doesn't meet your every need — which nearly no man will ever do.

Your guy doesn't get your full focus

That said, a dozen or more of the men I've gone out with have kept in contact with me even after we've decided we aren't a good match. However, none of them (to my knowledge) harbor any hope of our getting together again as sweethearts. It is clear we are just pals now and enjoy enough of the other to want to stay connected.

But I draw the line at doing anything date-like with any of them. If we have lunch together, it is Dutch treat. If we go to the movies or a hike, there is no hand holding, romantic touching nor smooching. If there were, that would be unfair to the man I've sworn exclusivity to as well as sending mixed signals to my pal.

You may also want to discuss this with your guy, as he, too, may have women he was seeing who want him to stay in touch. You should come up with a solution that feels right to both of you based on how you would feel if the situation was flipped. Would you be upset if you knew your guy was still in contact with women he was seeing before you and he decided to be exclusive? Most women would. But he may see nothing wrong with your continuing to pal around with these jilted guys, especially if they like to do things he doesn't (e.g., tennis, hiking, opera). However, he may not like it any more than you'd like him hanging with those he rejected for you.

The boyfriend phone

Give a prospective suitor only your cell phone number until you know him well enough to know he won't be a stalker. A cell phone number can't be traced easily to a street address, as a land line can.

Since few people other than potential or current suitors call me on my cell phone, I've begun referring to it as "the boyfriend phone." Sort of like the Bat Phone, but they get the Goddess rather than Batman. And while their needs may seem urgent to them, unlike Batman, rarely do I drop everything and fly to them. Their urgency passes once they take a cold shower or start doing their taxes.

Sort of like the Bat Phone, but they get the Goddess rather than Batman

Once we exchange numbers, I enter his into my cell phone. Then when/if he calls, I know who I'll be talking to, unless he's blocked his ID. If I'm with another guy, I turn off the ringer and don't answer. That would be rude!

Some people have ring tones specific to each guy. I could see "It Must Be Him" or "Some Enchanted Evening" or "Let's Get it On" linked to specific guys, depending on how I felt about him.

If you use your cell primarily for personal calls and potential beaus, consider only giving your first name in the outgoing message, again for your safety. It is so easy to Google you and find out where you live and a map to your house. There's no need to give more info than needed.

Keeping the man-funnel full

People often ask why I continue to communicate with new men after I've met one for coffee, or even accepted a second date. Why, they ask, don't I just stop communicating with others and stay focused on one at a time?

Dating is, to some degree, a numbers game.

Of course there are stories of people finding long-term happiness with the first person with whom they went out. Good for them! I'm even a tad envious of my divorced neighbor who met the sweetie she's been dating for 2 years after going out with only 8 other men in the previous 6 months.

I, on the other hand, have recently had a date with my ninety-first man. People ask me if I'm trying to get to number 100. I say, "No, I'm trying to get to number 92!" I'd be happy if the next man I met was The One. I have no need to try to reach some arbitrary number.

Knowing what I now know, I believe it's important to keep the man-funnel full — even if just partially full. That means that I continue responding to inquiries from men who meet my basic criteria. Right now I'm juggling 8 men via email, phone and IM. Some are potentially viable matches. Some are age or geographically undesirable but have something compelling about them, so we stay in touch. We've become flirtatious pen pals, knowing the likelihood we'll actually meet is pretty small.

Why keep your funnel full? If my numbers are any indication of the norm, only 10-20% of contacts will result in a face-to-face meeting. During the emailing or phoning stage one or both of you will decide there's no interest, so will say so directly or just stop communicating.

Why keep your funnel full?

Of those I met for coffee, twice as many were one-meeting encounters as those who warranted a second date.

So you keep your the man-stream flowing as so many drop out that if you only communicate with one at a time it will take a long time to find someone with enough mutual interest to see each other a second, let alone subsequent, time.

What if you find it difficult to get one man in your funnel, let alone multiples? If you're online, you may need to rewrite your profile, post more flattering pictures or adjust your criteria. (See "The man-sieve" in the *Assessing Your Assets: Why You're A Great Catch* book.)

And there's always the question of "How do you keep them all straight?" It is easy with my Date-A-Base (See page 7). One friend tracks those in his pipeline through a spreadsheet. Whatever you do, keep some notes, otherwise you'll ask the same questions you just asked in the previous conversation — which is a turn off!

What's your take on keeping the man-funnel full? Are you a one-at-a-time gal or do you embrace the funnel-full philosophy?

What's your definition of "committed"?

A friend told me he's going to buy a house with "Francine," a woman he's been seeing for a few years.

"Great!" I said. "You haven't cohabited with anyone for a long time, so this will be quite a change for you."

"No. I'll buy it with her and stay there sometimes, but I'll keep my place."

"Really? Why?"

"I don't want to give up my freedom."

Later in the conversation, he mentioned "Alice," another woman who he dated simultaneously when he started dating Francine. It became clear he was still seeing (and sleeping with) her, even

> *"I don't want to give up my freedom."*

though he was going to buy a house with Francine.

I was incredulous. Mustering all my self-control to use a non-judgmental voice, I said, "Based upon what you've told me about your relationship with Francine, if I were her I'd think we were in a committed monogamous relationship."

"We are in a committed relationship."

"But not a monogamous one. Does she know that?"

"She knows that I'm still in touch with Alice."

"But not that you're still sleeping with her?"

"She doesn't need to know that."

You could have picked up my chin from the table. "If I were Francine, I would definitely want to know about your relationship with Alice."

"She doesn't need to know that."

"No you wouldn't. She's happy thinking I'm 100% her man. I'm happy. She's happy. No problem."

I was speechless. Knowing there was nothing I could say that would dissuade him from his thinking he was in the right, I gave up.

I wonder how many of us have been with a man

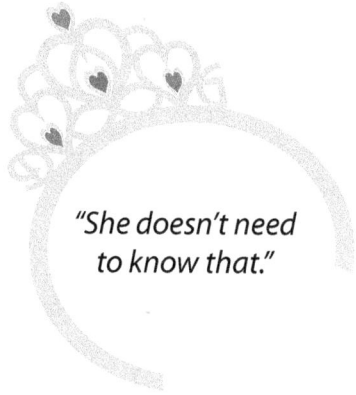

who claimed to be exclusive and committed and yet he had another woman on the side. I had that experience once. The challenge is, you rarely have enough hard evidence to know for sure.

In fact, this guy told me Francine had found evidence of another woman in his apartment. When she asked about it, he told the truth — up to a point. He didn't lie, but he didn't tell everything. She didn't probe, content with his flimsy explanation.

An author of a book about cheating was asked why people cheat. The answer was, "Because they can."

It's bad enough that when we don't ask the hard questions we live in a fantasyland, some of which is our own making. But the hard reality is it's doubtful that this philanderer practices safe sex, so is putting these women at risk.

Do we fool ourselves? Do we believe what we want to believe? Do we put up with flimsy excuses because we don't want to rock the boat, or accuse someone we love of infidelity?

Another one bites the dust

With apologies to Queen (but without the violence of their song), I share that another one bites the dust. Number 102. The result of my latest foray into Match.com.

After a few email exchanges, we talked for an hour and I mentioned the next evening I was going to a public street fair within walking distance of my house. He said, "I may go to that and look for you." Uh huh. Great way to set up something certain, as 30,000 people attend this event.

He called me from the event and asked if I was there yet. I said I was leaving in 15 minutes. He said he'd "look for me." Right. In a crowd of thousands you're going to find someone you've never met. I didn't press for a more certain location, as I figured he must not be too interested if he didn't want to set a specific spot.

Ten minutes later he called to say he was in a nice bar and had a table. Finally, some certainty! A plan!

What a concept. I said I'd be there in a few minutes.

He was smart, tall, educated and successful. But I'm afraid we just didn't have enough in common. In fact, we are polar opposites politically, not that I don't enjoy a spirited discussion. But I'm not fond of arguments that aren't likely to yield either of us changing our opinions.

He wasn't odious or disrespectful and even bought me a glass of wine. But his regular interjection of curse words and his repeating himself grew tiring. He did ask me a few questions, and I interjected my thoughts when he didn't.

The drink evolved to a light dinner at an inexpensive ethnic restaurant down the street. When the bill came, I got out my wallet, as my male buddies have coached me to do on a first encounter. He said my share was $14. OK. That's usually a screaming sign that there's no interest in a repeat rendezvous.

We walked back to where our destinations required a split. He hugged me and said, "Talk to you soon." Which generally means, "Have a nice life." Which is okay, as I wasn't really feeling it either.

One of the hardest things about midlife dating is keeping your optimism in the face of a number of going-nowhere encounters. The interaction isn't horrible, it's just not great. Ambivalence. It's the all-too-common reality of this exercise. So I keep my hopes up and respond to the next man knocking on my in-box.

Expensive gifts too soon

I would have never predicted that this would be a problem in dating. But it was — for a friend of mine.

She was dating a few guys casually. On the fourth date with one, he bought her a large flat screen computer monitor. When asked why, he told her, "Because you need it."

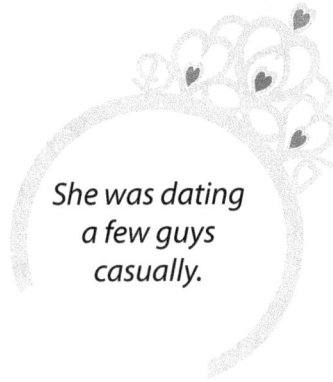

She was dating a few guys casually.

He did not get it on sale or discount. He is not a wealthy man, but isn't impoverished either. She had not mentioned she longed for a large monitor. He noticed her smaller one and went out and bought it.

Normally, we'd adore a man who saw something that would improve our lives and acted on it — even without our mentioning it. But since this was only their fourth date, it was too much too soon. Besides, she wasn't really interested in continuing to see him. She had no intention of accepting such an expensive gift (nearly $1000), but what if she had, then broke it off with him soon after? Not good for either party.

Some women say, "Hey, a man feels good about taking care of a woman, buying her presents he knows she'll appreciate. So what if she stops seeing him? He'll have had the joy of knowing he's made her happy."

While it's true most men like to make a woman they care about happy, it's also true that they can feel taken advantage of. Many men have complained to me about women who just see them as a walking wallet. But is this scenario different since she didn't ask for, nor even mention wanting, a larger monitor?

I think other-than-small gifts early in a relationship can be trouble. I've received many small gifts from men I'm starting to date, but nothing over $50. Some were items I appreciated; others were just something the man picked up thinking any woman would like it. I'm not just any woman, so I'm generally hard to buy for. But I always appreciated his thoughtfulness and effort.

A suitor in every (air)port

My mother would refer to a single, traveling ladies' man as someone who "had a girl in every port." Just like many of the sailors she knew as a young woman.

Now, as a traveling woman yet to find a local man I want to date regularly, I'm finding I have gentlemen in various parts of the country. I saw a favorite for a drink in his local airport hotel bar during a 2-hour layover yesterday.

> *I have gentlemen in various parts of the country*

Another picked me up from his nearby airport, took me for a drink and delivered me to my hotel. One took me to dinner and dancing near his home base. Another fetched me from an out-of-town client engagement and drove me to my friend's home 5 hours away. We had a fun time during the journey getting to know each other better than we had on the phone.

While I'm not an advocate of getting in the car of a man I haven't met, I'd been talking to each of these guys for a while. So even though I yearn for a local man to enjoy local events, if a geographically undesirable man is interesting enough, I'll accept his invitation to get together if I know I'll be in his area.

I'm careful to set boundaries and not lead him to think that I'm looking for a 1-night stand, nor is our distance-challenged situation optimal. I've tried long-distance relationships and I find that visiting each other every few weeks just doesn't let us get to know each other in the way I want.

Am I as guilty of being a "player" like the sailors my mother referenced? Since I'm honest and transparent, I don't feel I'm being duplicitous. If we both enjoy each other's company and don't try to take advantage of the other, then there's no harm. Hurt happens when one begins to have more feelings than the other, but that can happen in any relationship, whether local or not.

Have you tried meeting singles out of your area?

Resources

Make sure to download your free eBook Attract Your Next Great Mate: Dating Advice From Top Relationship Experts *at www. DatingGoddess.com/freebie*

Afterword

At the time of this writing, I have not yet found my true King Charming. I continue my search with verve. I've become more discerning about what I want and don't want. I've met some wonderful men pals — my treasures — who continue to be in touch.

I wish you much luck in your adventure. It will be fun and frustrating, exhilarating and exasperating, and sexy or sexless. So much depends on you, your approach and your attitude. My books are designed to help you enjoy as much as possible and ward off unpleasantness. But nearly all adventures have wonderful highs as well as a few lows. If you know that going in and arm yourself with information on what to expect, you'll have more of the positives and fewer of the negatives.

Please drop by www.DatingGoddess.com and join in the discussion and report on your experiences.

Dating Goddess

Resources

o to www.datinggoddess.com to access a variety of useful resources. We work to suggest resources we think have value.

Dating and relationship book reviews

These reviews will save you time and money as I've given you my take on specific books, CDs and more. Some are worth your effort to buy and read or listen to them — some are not. We're always adding new book reviews, so check frequently. We'll also notify our mailing list when new resources are added.

Dating site links

There are a lot of dating sites on the Internet. I've listed the ones I think are worth investigating.

Dating products and tools

Dating can be daunting. We're continually looking at

ways to make it easier and more fun. We'll provide info on games, tools, even date-wear that will help others know you're available, or help you get to know potential suitors better.

Dating and relationship advice sites

Advice "experts" abound on the Internet as anyone can self-proclaim themseves as expert — even if they haven't dated in 30 years and never in midlife. I've worked to find experts who's advice I generally think is solid.

Midlife recources

We'll feature Web sites, books, events and other resources we think might interest you.

Newly discovered resources

I'll add other resources as we discover them, subscribe to our mailing list to get the scoop as soon as we find them. Go to www.DatingGoddess.com to register for our mailing list. Don't worry, we won't sell or give your email to anyone.

Acknowledgments

Let me start by acknowledging the 112 men who helped trigger the lessons contained in this book. Some prompted several! They remain nameless here to protect their identity, although most would recognize references to them. Plus the thousands more whose winks, emails and calls didn't result in a date, but helped me learn the dating game. And all those men who I emailed who never responded — such a blessing to have them weed themselves out.

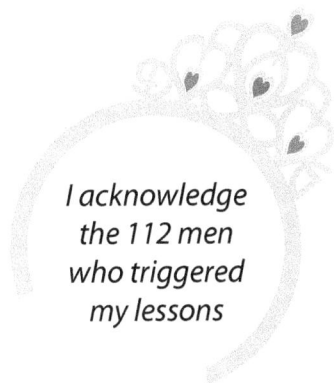

> I acknowledge the 112 men who triggered my lessons

I'd like to thank my Seven Sisters mastermind group for the tremendous brainstorming, noodling, strategizing and encouragement. I wouldn't have begun this project without the prodding of Val Cade, Chris Clarke-Epstein, Mariah Burton Nelson, Sue Dyer, Sam Horn and Marilynn Mobley.

Thank you to my good friends who've listened to my dating stories ad nauseam, and whose support and wisdom are embedded in this text. Ed Betts, Ken Braly, Bruce Daley, Tom Drews, Elaine Floyd, Paulette Ensign, Scott Friedman, Craig Harrison, Mary Jansen, Tom Johnson, Sandy Jones, Mary Kilkenny, Ellie Klevins, Patrick Lynch, Mary Marcdante, Barbara McNichol, Ann Peterson, Anthony Ramsey, Caterina Rando, Kristy Rogers, Jana Stanfield, Holly Stiel, Terry Tepliz, and George Walther, thank you.

The Adventures in Delicious Dating After 40 series

The *Adventures in Delicious Dating After 40* series is designed to help you understand your own midlife dating journey. It is not a road map, as we all take different routes. It is a guide to help you understand yourself, midlife men, and the dating process. Hopefully, you'll not only learn from the lessons and insights shared in this series, but you'll examine how they apply — or don't — to your own dating adventure.

You'll get the scoop on what you need to know, what's changed since you last dated, and how to navigate inevitable bumps in the road.

Following is an overview of each book in the series and a sampling of some of the chapter titles. All are detailed at www.DatingGoddess.com.

Date or Wait: Are You Ready for Mr. Great?

Are you ready for a special man in your life? You have a great life. But you know you'd like a special man to share it. You think you're ready to date, but you haven't done it in a while.

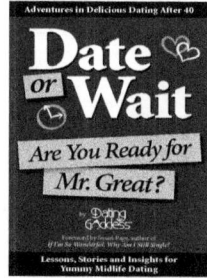

What should you consider before you actually start dating full bore? Even if you've reentered the dating world, this will give you a foundation of attitude and philosophy to make your adventure more fulfilling.

Sample chapters

💜 From hurt to flirt

💜 Dating is like Baskin-Robbins

💜 You've got to kiss a lot of…princes!

💜 What's your definition of dating success?

💜 Are you open to receiving?

💜 Dating: A self-designed personal-growth workshop

💜 Hands-on dating research

💜 Being present to the presents

💜 Being aggressively single

💜 Approaching dating like a buffet

💜 Is Brad Pitt ruining your love life?

💜 Treasures can come in dented packages

Assessing Your Assets: Why You're A Great Catch

You have many wonderful qualities. But it's easy to focus on one's flaws — at least what seem like flaws to you. However, to the right man your imperfections are endearing, attractive and lovable. You have to be clear what you offer a man who will find you enchanting.

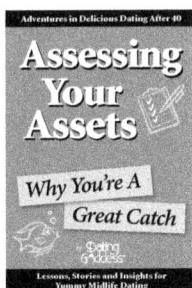

Assessing Your Assets helps you look at what you bring to a new relationship. It will help you see your good points so you'll approach dating with more confidence.

Sample chapters

💜 Don't think you are damaged goods

💜 You are (probably) more attractive than you think!

💜 They aren't called "hate handles"

💜 Are you a good man picker?

💜 What are your deal breakers?

💜 Are you arguing your limitations?

💜 Turn your liabilities into assets

💜 The strong vs. nice woman debate

💜 Is your sense of humor stunting your dating?

💜 Why are we drawn to bad boys?

💜 The zest test

In Search of King Charming: Who Do I Want to Share My Throne?

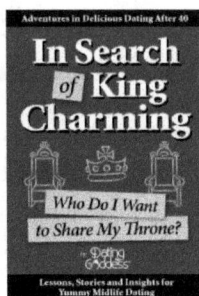

You are no longer looking for "Prince" Charming because you are a queen. You want someone who is at your level, not groveling at your feet. You want a king — someone who's your equal and with whom you can rule the throne together!

This book focuses on helping you better define what you want beyond tall, dark and handsome! You'll consider characteristics you might not have thought of before. You'll look at what you want now.

Sample chapters

💚 Building your Franken-boyfriend

💚 What's your "perfect boyfriend's" job description?

💚 A man to go with your wardrobe

💚 In search of the elusive good kisser

💚 When you're clear on what you want, it appears

💚 Are you dating the same guy in different bodies?

💚 Does he fit in your world?

💚 What's your kissing quotient?

💚 Is your guy's loving muscle strong?

💚 Do you both have the same dating rhythm?

Embracing Midlife Men:
Insights Into Curious Behaviors

Do you sometimes scratch your head after interacting with a midlife man, wondering, "What could he possibly be thinking?" Especially if it's before, during or after a date with a man who presumably wants to impress you!

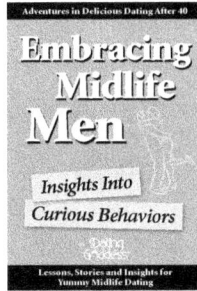

This book focuses on better understanding midlife men's behaviors. When you grasp what's going on in his head it's much easier to embrace him. Men are wondrous creatures, so we need to understand them better and love them for who they are.

Sample chapters

💚 Men are like shoes

💚 Why men disappear when it gets serious

💚 Chivalry isn't dead —but it seems to be hibernating

💚 Do men want feisty women?

💚 Midlife men have forgotten how to date

💚 Are you getting prime time from your man?

💚 When a man tells you what he paid for things

💚 Does he treat you like his ex?

💚 Has Greg Behrendt done women a disservice?

💚 Tales of woo

Dipping Your Toe in the Dating Pool: Dive In Without Belly Flopping

You've decided you are ready — you want to start dating. Maybe you've already had a few coffee dates with several men. You want to be as successful as possible on your dating adventure.

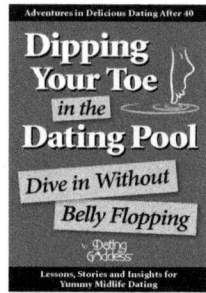

This book focuses on getting started on your dating adventures. We cover what you need to know as you begin your journey.

Sample chapters

♥ Do you have the right datewear?

♥ Dating with integrity

♥ Building your rejection muscle

♥ When "be yourself" is questionable advice

♥ Faux beaus and practice dating

♥ Are you making bad decisions out of loneliness?

♥ Being "in wonder" about your date's behavior

♥ When do you feel most vulnerable in dating?

♥ Are you out of his league — or he yours?

♥ Why listening is so seductive

Winning at the Online Dating Game: Stack the Deck in Your Favor

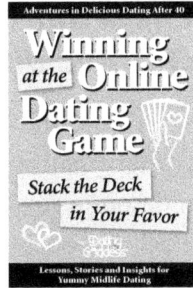

Internet dating can be frustrating or fruitful. It will be much less exasperating if you know how to read and weed out men's profiles that aren't appropriate for you. And you'll have a steady stream of potential suitors if you know how to write a compelling profile for yourself.

This book focuses on the ins and outs of online dating. How to play the game, which has it's own rules and language. If you don't understand how online dating works, you'll waste a lot of time connecting with men who are not a possible fit for you.

Sample chapters

💚 Shopping for men

💚 Safe online dating

💚 Is 21st Century dating unnatural?

💚 What do men look at in your profile?

💚 Euphemisms uncovered

💚 Are you describing yourself compellingly?

💚 No, I will not be dating your Harley

💚 Playing the online dating game

💚 Scantily clothed pictures

Check Him Out Before Going Out: Avoiding Dud Dates

Under the cloak of the anonymity that email and the phone provides, men often reveal more than they intend. If you ask the right questions you can find out a lot about his values and view of the world after just an interaction or two.

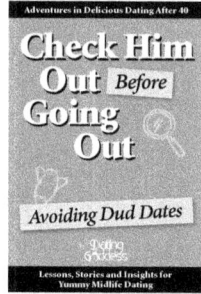

This book focuses on what you need to ask before agreeing to even a coffee date. You need to vet the men who email and call you to ensure you're not likely to waste your time with men who clearly aren't a match.

Sample chapters

💚 Becoming smitten with the fantasy

💚 Can Google help — or hinder — your dating life?

💚 Qualify your potential dates before meeting

💚 The art of consideration

💚 Anticipating a big date is like awaiting Santa

💚 Being seduced by what he is over who he is

💚 Are you his spare?

💚 My boyfriend, whom I haven't met

💚 When canceling is the right thing to do

💚 Politics, religion and sex — oh my!

First-Rate First Dates: Increasing the Chances of a Second Date

You can tell a lot about someone within the first 30 minutes. What does he talk about? Does he ask you questions? If so, what does he want to know about you? What do you need to know about him? How does he treat you? How does he treat those around you?

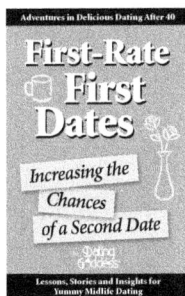

This book focuses on what goes on during the first date. How do you determine if you want a second date? What you can do to increase the likelihood your date will ask you for a second? That is if you want a repeat!

Sample chapters

💗 Start with coffee

💗 How do you greet him?

💗 When it clicks, throw out some of your criteria

💗 Tracking your date's score

💗 Clues a guy is just looking for a booty call

💗 12 signs he won't be asking for a second date

💗 First-date red flags that this guy isn't for you

💗 Honesty is not always the best policy

💗 Chemistry, or does he make my toes curl?

💗 Women's first-date blunders

Real Deal or Faux Beau: Should You Keep Seeing Him?

You've begun to go out with a man you like. How do you decide if you should continue seeing him, or if you should release him because he's not The One?

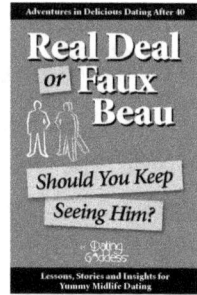

This book focuses on second dates and beyond. During the dating process you are both assessing if you want to keep seeing each other. This book helps you determine what questions you need to ask yourself.

Sample chapters

💚 Deciding to see him again or not

💚 What's your date's Delight/Disappointment Scale score?

💚 Broaching tough conversations

💚 "I want to respect me in the morning"

💚 Does he invite you to his place?

💚 Are you stingy in dating?

💚 When his hand is on your knee too soon

💚 Easy way to ask hard questions

💚 Rose-colored glasses obscure red flags

💚 If his stories don't add up, subtract yourself

Multidating Responsibly: Play the Field Without Being A Player

Playing the field is frowned on in some circles. There are definitely appropriate and inappropriate ways to date several men simultaneously.

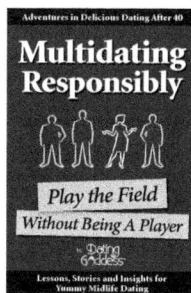

This book focuses on how to date around responsibly and with integrity without leading men on. If you do it with honesty, you can date several people at once until you're both ready to focus only on each other.

Sample chapters

💜 "Pimpin'" — Dating multiple guys

💜 Multi-dating pros and cons

💜 Your Date-A-Base — tracking multiple suitors

💜 "Hot bunking" your beaus

💜 Are you a "Let's Make a Deal" type of dater?

💜 Assume there are other women

💜 Dating's revolving door

💜 How long do you hedge your bet?

💜 Beware of multi-tasking when multi-dating

💜 Back burner beaus

💜 The boyfriend phone

69

Moving On Gracefully: Break Up Without Heartache

"Breaking up" sounds so high school, doesn't it? But part of the dating process is saying something when one of you decides not to date the other anymore. Going "poof" is not a mature or respectful option in midlife.

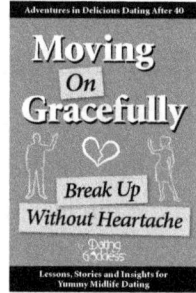

This book focuses on surviving a breakup, whether you initiate it or not. Either way, it's never easy to break up if you have developed any fondness toward the other.

Sample chapters

💜 Hello — goodbye: How to say no thanks after meeting

💜 Releasing back into the dating pool

💜 50 ways to leave your lover? 4 ways not to leave your suitor

💜 Breaking up is hard to do — right

💜 Why men go "poof"

💜 How to trump being dumped

💜 When breaking up is a "Get Out of Jail Free" card

💜 How to detect the end is near

💜 Failed relationships' blessings

💜 He's broken up with you — he just didn't tell you

💜 Rejection is protection

From Fear to Frolic: Get Naked Without Getting Embarrassed

This book focuses on what you need to consider and know before getting physically intimate with a man you're dating. This is nerve-wracking to many midlife women. This book will prepare you.

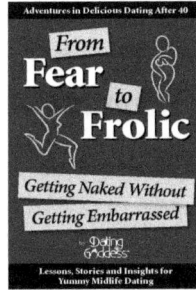

Sample chapters

💜 Sleepover do's and don'ts

💜 Does he want in your life — or just in your bedroom?

💜 Getting naked with him the first time

💜 An excuse to seduce or how important is bedroom bliss?

💜 What to ask yourself before getting naked with him

💜 Are you and your guy on the same sexual time line?

💜 Sharing your sexual owner's manual with him

💜 What women need from a man before having sex

💜 Why too-soon midlife sex is like non-fat food

💜 How dating sex is like waffles

💜 Too-soon seduction: "I'm special, but not THAT special"

Ironing Out Dating Wrinkles: Work Through Challenges Without Getting Steamed

Nearly all relationships have some ups and downs. Part of getting to know someone is knowing how they work through relationship misunderstandings.

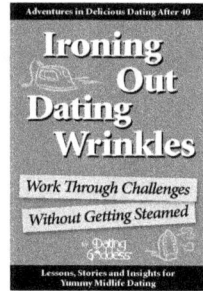

This book focuses on how to work through the inevitable hiccups that happen when you are getting to know each other. If you can both deal with challenges, the bond deepens and you find yourself smitten.

Sample chapters

💜 When your guy vexes you, ask what your highest self would do

💜 The first fight

💜 You want boo; he wants boo-ty

💜 Where's the line between getting your needs met and being selfish?

💜 Expressing your upset with your guy

💜 Is his toothbrush in your cabinet too soon?

💜 Do you love how he loves you?

💜 Is he collecting data on how to make you happy?

💜 Be careful of being smitten

💜 Exclusivity: How and when to broach it

www.ingramcontent.com/pod-product-compliance
Lightning Source LLC
Chambersburg PA
CBHW071245020426
42333CB00015B/1643